ABC
Science
Experiments

Harry Milgrom
Director of Science
New York City Public Schools

illustrated by
Donald Crews

Crowell-Collier Press
Collier-Macmillan Limited, London

Library of Congress Catalog Card Number: 75-116788

The Macmillan Company
866 Third Avenue, New York, New York 10022

Collier-Macmillan Canada Ltd., Toronto, Ontario

Printed in the United States of America

First Printing

A Message to Parents and Teachers

On the day a baby is born, he begins his search for an understanding of the world around him. At first his explorations are confined to a world of small dimensions. As he grows older and his powers of perception develop, his search moves outward in ever-spreading ripples. By poking and probing, by looking and listening, by feeling and tasting, he trys to bring some order to the chaos of impressions that bombard him. When the child is able to talk he starts questioning. Many an adult has been worn to a frazzle trying to keep pace with the lively mind of a curious child.

During the child's early years, parents and teachers can help the child grow in understanding by providing opportunities for him to obtain simple answers to his questions through firsthand investigation; by introducing him to experiences that stir new wonderment; and by creating an atmosphere in which he will feel free to question and explore, to make his own discoveries and to work out his own explanations.

Starting at the early age of four, three or even two, a child can be given practice in the techniques of finding out. Through selected activities, his faculties for observing and reasoning can be exercised. As these activities strengthen his feeling of wonderment, his zest for exploration, his power of imagination, his joy of anticipation and his thrill of discovery, the child gradually becomes filled with the true spirit of scientific inquiry, the spirit that hopefully will remain with him and inspire all learning for the rest of his life.

ABC Science Experiments is a pictorial guide to investigations in science that can be carried out by preschool children.

It is designed to alert children to the simple wonders all around them and to show them what they can find out about these wonders.

It is designed to provide the experiences in which the seeds of scientific interest and understanding can take root and grow.

The material in this book is arranged in three parts:

1. For each investigation, a picture and simple text show the child what to do.
2. A basic question asks the child to explain what he observes.
3. A section at the back of the book gives answers and other information.

Let the child ask questions freely. Let the child give his own answers and explanations freely. Encourage him to look for things to explore and to suggest what he would like to try. In other words, establish an atmosphere in which the child can exercise a most important freedom—the freedom to speculate, think and reason.

A air

**Blow air through
a straw
onto your hand.**

Can you feel
the air?
Can you hear it?
Can you see it?

B ball

**Hold the ball high.
Let go.**

**What does
the ball do?**

C cup

Float a cup in water. Put pennies in the cup.

What happens to the cup?

D drop

Sprinkle some water on waxed paper.

What happens to the water?

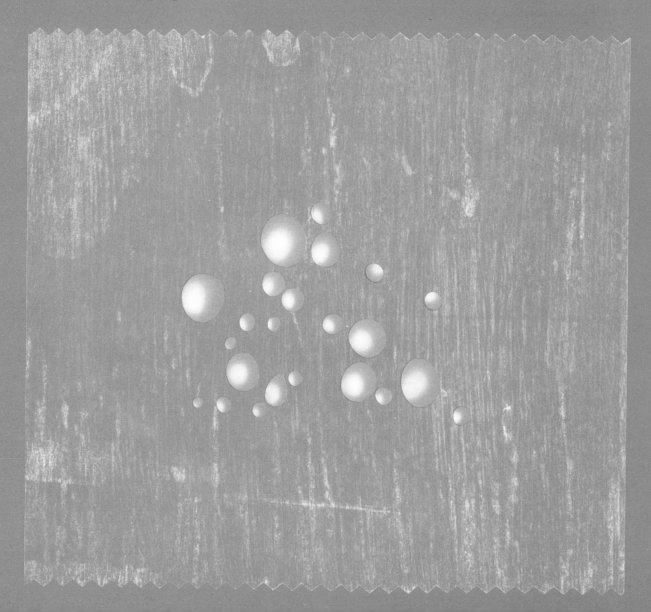

E egg

Stand a hard-boiled egg on its end. Let go.

What happens to the egg?

F fork

Hang a fork
from a string.
Let the fork
hit the edge
of the table.

What do you hear?

G glove

Wear an old glove on your right hand. Hold an ice cube in each hand.

Which hand feels cold first?

H hoop

Push a hoop.

What does the
hoop do?

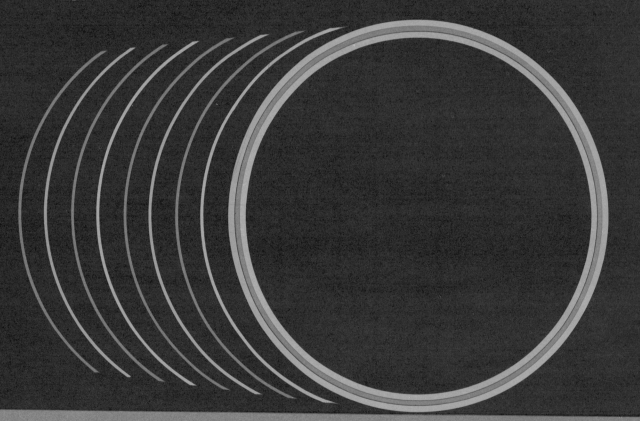

I ice

Put an ice cube in a dish. Let it stand for a while.

What happens to the ice?

J jet

Make a jet flyer.
Blow up a long
balloon. Let go of it.

What does
the balloon do?

K key

Try to pick up different kinds of keys with a magnet.

Which ones does the magnet lift?

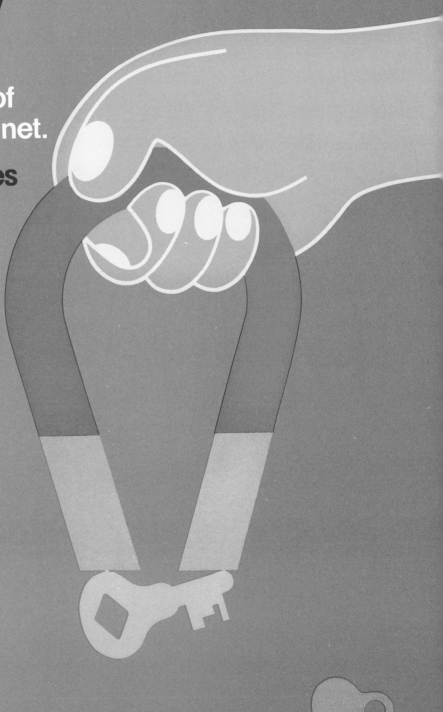

L light

Hold your hand
in sunlight.

What do you see?

M magnet

Line up some paper clips.

How many paper clips can your magnet pull?

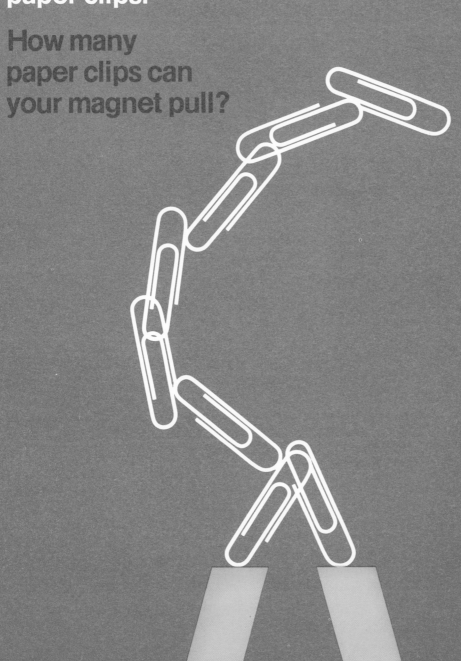

N nail

**Make a mark
with nail polish
at the base of
your nail.
Leave the polish on
for a few days.**

Where is the mark
after a few days?

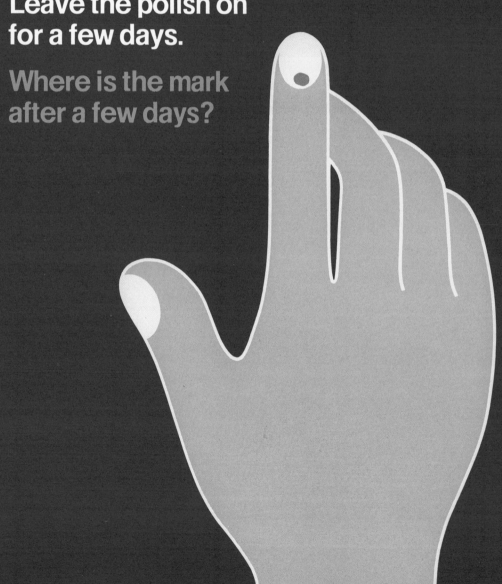

O oil

Put some water in a glass. Add some cooking oil.

What happens to the oil?

P pencil

Try to write on waxed paper with a pencil.

What happens?

Q quarter

Spin a quarter on a table.

What do you hear?

R rock

Look at a rock through a magnifying glass.

What do you see?

S straw

Place a straw in water.
Hold your finger tightly
on the top end. Lift the
straw out of the water.

What happens to the
water in the straw?

220196

T top

Spin a top.

**When does the top
fall and stop?**

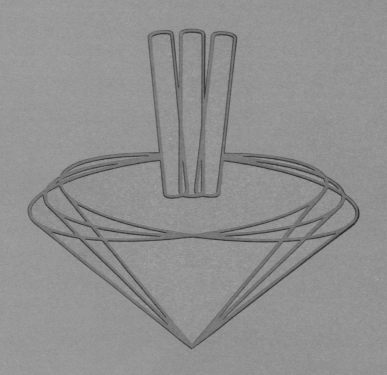

U universe

**Look up at the sky
on a clear night.**

What can you see?

V vortex

Form a vortex. Let
water run out of a sink.

**What does the water
do as it runs out?**

W water

Put some drops
of red food coloring
in a glass of water.

What happens
to the red color?

X xylophone

**Hit a long bar.
Hit a short bar.**

Which bar makes
the higher sound?

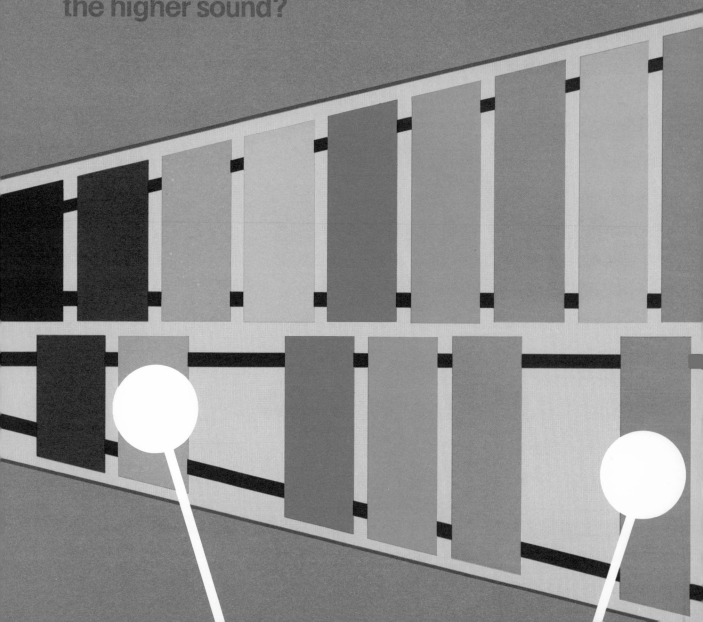

Y yo-yo

Let a yo-yo go.

**What does the
yo-yo do as it falls?**

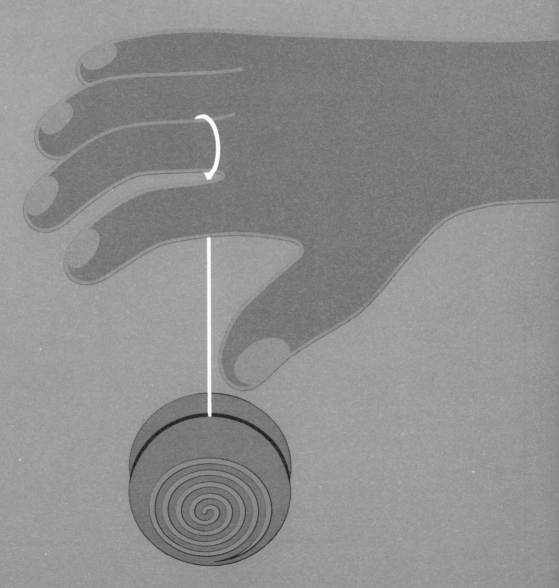

Z zipper

Zip a zipper.

Why does the zipper stay together when it is closed?

Notes for Parents and Teachers

For your guidance, suggested answers and other bits of related information are presented in this section. Undoubtedly, your child will come up with a variety of responses, all of which should be treated with respect. A measure of the success of the ABC activities will be the extent to which he looks for new things to explore, observe and seek to explain.

A air
You can feel moving air. You can hear air as it moves out of the straw. However, you cannot see air. Basically, air is a mixture of two invisible gases, oxygen and nitrogen. Since air is matter in the gaseous state, it has weight and can push against things. Air also takes up space.

B ball
As soon as the ball is released it begins to move down—that is, it falls. Every object is attracted by the earth's gravity. When an object is free to fall, the force of gravity pulls it "down"—that is, toward the center of the earth.

C cup
As more and more pennies are put into the cup, it sinks deeper and deeper into the water. The cup floats at a depth where the weight of water that the cup pushes aside is equal to its own weight. With increasing weight due to the pennies, the cup has to sink deeper to continue to push aside its own weight of water. The limit is reached when water enters the cup. It becomes heavy enough then to sink to the bottom of the container.

D drop
On waxed paper, water rolls up into drops of different sizes. Water does not seep into the waxed paper. As a result, each sprinkle of water pulls itself together to form a drop. Large drops are heavier and therefore flatter than small drops. When two drops touch, they fuse into one larger drop.

E egg
When the egg is released, it rolls over and comes to rest on its side. If the egg were perfectly balanced on one end, it might remain upright. Since the egg is not in perfect balance, gravity pulls it down to the lowest possible position, which is the position when the egg is on its side.

F fork
The fork gives off a sound when it hits the table, because the force of the impact makes the tines of the fork vibrate, or move back and forth. The vibrating tines produce the sound. Forks of different sizes will emit different sounds.

G glove
The left hand feels cold first. The glove on the right hand stops the flow of heat from the right hand to the ice. In other words, the glove is a heat insulator. Hence the right hand retains its heat and stays warm. The unprotected left hand loses its heat to the ice and feels cold.

H hoop
The hoop rolls when it is pushed. The hoop has the shape of a circle. Of all geometric shapes, the circle is the one that rolls on a surface with the greatest ease. Of course, it is this roundness that gives the wheel its great importance in land transportation.

I ice
The ice in the dish melts into water. Ice is the solid state that water can assume at temperatures of 32°F. or below. At room temperatures of more than 32°F, ice melts and becomes liquid water again.

J jet
Upon release, a jet of air pushes out of the balloon's mouth. As the air escapes, the balloon darts around the room in a helter-skelter manner. This illustrates one of Newton's laws of motion, "For every action, there is an equal and opposite reaction."

K key
If the magnet lifts the key, the key is made of, or contains, iron. If the magnet does not lift the key, it does not contain iron. In that case the key may be made of brass, aluminum or another nonmagnetic material.

L light
You can see the shadow of the hand. It forms when light is blocked by an object through which light cannot pass. A shadow is an area that is not reached by the light.

M magnet
The number of paper clips that a magnet can pull gives a measure of the strength of the magnet. The stronger the magnet, the longer the train of clips the magnet can haul.

N nail
After a few days the mark on the nail is above the base. As new nail tissue grows, the old dead tissue is pushed out of the finger. The movement of the polish mark shows at what rate the nail grows.

O oil
The oil floats on top of the water because of two basic characteristics. First, oil is less dense than water. Second, oil does not mix with water. It is possible to disperse oil in water for a short time by shaking the mixture vigorously. When the shaking stops, however, the oil runs together and floats back to the top.

P pencil
The pencil does not write on waxed paper. In order to leave a mark, the graphite ("lead") of the pencil must rub off on the paper. The waxed paper is too smooth. Hence, no graphite rubs off on it.

Q quarter
At first the quarter spins silently. When it begins to fall, it rattles against the table faster and faster. The pitch of the sound rises. When the quarter comes to rest flat on the table, the sound stops.

R rock
You see many different bits of mineral matter of various colors and shapes. Some are arranged in layers. Some are shiny, some dull.

S straw
The water stays in the straw. As long as the top of the straw is kept closed with the finger, the water cannot run out. As soon as you take the finger off the top of the straw, the water runs out. In the first case, air cannot enter the straw so the water cannot leave it. In the second case, air enters through the top and the water falls.

T top
The top falls and stops when the spinning stops. As long as the top spins rapidly, it remains upright. As the top slows, it begins to fall. The friction at the point increases. The top slows even more. Then, the top falls on its side and the spinning comes to a halt.

U universe
On a clear night, when there are no tall trees, buildings or mountains obstructing the view, you can see half of the universe. You can see the stars, planets, the Milky Way galaxy and nebulae. At times you can also see meteors, comets and the moon.

V vortex
As water goes down the drain, it spins around to form a vortex. A similar vortex in a large body of water is called a whirlpool. In air, a vortex may result in a whirlwind, a hurricane or a tornado.

W water
The red color gradually spreads throughout the water. When the red is evenly distributed, it is said to be "in solution" in the water.

X xylophone
The short bar gives off the higher sound. The shorter the length of the vibrating material, the higher the pitch of the sound. The longer the length, the lower the sound.

Y yo-yo
As the yo-yo falls, it spins around faster and faster. At the bottom of the string the yo-yo is spinning fast enough to make it climb back up the string to the starting position.

Z zipper
When the zipper is closed, it is held together by little interlocking hooks on each side of the zipper. These hooks are pried apart by the slide when the zipper is opened.